SPACE PARSLEY

BY KAT ADDIS

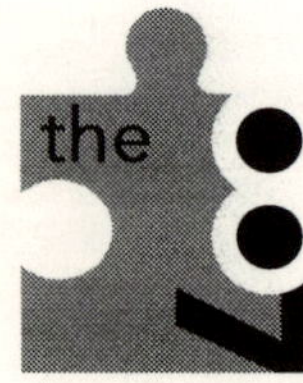

Published 2021 by the87press

The 87 Press LTD

87 Stonecot Hill

Sutton

Surrey

SM3 9HJ

www.the87press.com

ISBN: 978-1-8380698-6-5

Cover Design: Ella Mahony

Typesetting: Stanislava Stoilova [www.sdesign.graphics]

for Bea and Joe

A POEM OF CONTENTS

1.

You'll hear me when you're listening to me

simplesse oblige

I've made a young mistake so I can watch it grow up
rigorously, into another man from the woman that I am now
the different kinds of crying and reasoning are so boring
        between rolling hopes there's a vague pain, and a cliff.
                    From my lovers
I expected pity but not to be forgiven.
I am old now, not like all the reliable people
                            beans for a long time, soft waves
        parts of myself that make me ashamed
and I am ashamed, of the vanity and the fruit
            and my loss of thoughts and the clear broth of splash
that whatever pleases the world is a stiff drink

2.

because I wanted to cut the crap on my vendetta
and punish a thousand men in one blow
I took up my bow quickly
like the man who circulates in a dark time and place
it was my power or my virtue to the restrained heart
to make frosty and in her eyes diffuse
when the quickened body goes down there
where every single ray of sunlight is extinguished
but rolled over at the first assault
I had never enough power nor enough space.
I cannot arm myself at will
or be true to the tall and tiring tower
or hide myself quickly from the sharp cut
of whatever I desire today, and I can't help myself.

3.

That day the sunlight
        turned pale with pity
I was all tied up but I didn't know
        it was a woman that bound me (it was you)
time was not on my side
        but I went boldly,   WHALE!
I went without suspicion to the common
        where my struggle was due to commence.
They found me there without my shell on
        devalved my heart and tunnelled my eyes.
The way was wet and empty with tears.
        It does them no credit
to wound me like this. (When you arrived
        you had your weapon concealed.)

4.

She knows something about infinity, luck, and art
her unbelievable majesty shows in two shades of blue
gliding between this and that other hemisphere.
A whale is a kind of belief. She serves no gods.
Vegetables in the earth light up the menu
flying for many years has already iced up the truth.
Touch Giovanni on the reticence of Piero
and they'll do their bit to write it in the skies.
Writing cookbooks in Rome is a thankless task
if you don't parse the salt. She is so much the sovereign
                                        has-been
humiliation only makes it more arousing.
The sun bakes itself completely into this little hamlet
clumsily wanting to thank the place
where the bluest whale in the world was conceived.

5.

I'm calling you in sighs and whispers
the whale that I have scratched on my heart.
Now whining begins to break out of me: steam
I am crumbling bread, those first sweet sounds
the clock, the time, the altered existence we confront
my blue bravery swells up to the highest height:
uncover your curls of ambergris, so the entire world
Enough! What's good is for others more than for you and you
                                      are nobody!
I whine some more and then alter the lesson
to her own voice. "Let others call you. Even when
every reverence and honour is given
to Apollo, the upshot is piles of corpses."
I put an egg into the green ramekin,
a dead tongue elongates presumptuously in the wind

6.

if the worker and his madness wants me
to follow something blue that twists and turns
and at the same time run from a punishment I hardly
                              understand
although my running is slow and nightmarish
and however much I call out to the messenger ahead
only the men in the solid street listen to me
it seems pointless to leap at it or make it turn
for I am treacle-footed
indeed I am a horse! reigns force me to remember myself
I must remain within his mastery. O, a horse and its body
which in spite of my shout transports me to death
which is only a tree where we gather
whichever bitter fruit pleases others (or prays to them)
which, tasting, afflicts me more than it doesn't comfort

7.

the throat and the sound is the ozone lung:
it's the year of the world when power disbands
waves run in the tracks of my hesitance
our nature stands defeated in a wine-coloured costume.
Orpheus, are you exhausted, my kindly whale in the spume?
I designed my human life according to shapes in the sky
but it kept adding things that were hard to believe. Foppery.
Who wants to hide in the Helikon? Not your bloody hands.
What of the steam-powered laurel, the mechanical myrtle?
"There she goes, Lady Philosophy, poor and naked."
This was whispered when I won the village in a game of dice.
If I had taken the way of the whale I'd have even less company
                                        now.
I might have prayed for more, but before all that I looked back.
It only goes to show, the river runs under the magnificence of
                                        my song.

8.

At the foot of the hill where the beautiful view
goes sneaking under the skin of the land
Donna, the whale you're obsessed with, sends you on your way
often stooping to the sound of weeping (these sad roots).
To be free, to be in peace, we can all bang our drum for that
a life that will end when you die, with a cymbal crash
without fear of encountering on the path a wandering friar
who might devastate your journey with his capable hands.
But we are "seeds from a different packet"
which explains the differing state of our growth.
You over there serenely, you might be death.
(After all, this campaign is his,
the one that bench-presses in extremis
and stays sinewy and slow even in the major key)

leeve
mooder,
leet me in!

9.

It is spring when the planet checks the time,
returning from her power-holiday with Taurus.
A floret falls from the inflamed cauliflower
and decks out the world in a new colour.
And not even the ones who opened up the forests,
the rivers and the hills, pinked with buds like a jerkin
stay inside. We've already not met up in the park.
A heavy weight makes itself out of the earthly mood
in which such a fruit and such a s/i/mile congeals.
This is the way, between the women and the sun,
eat your granola, do your work, bright eyes
what else to do but clap a cry of love? Thoughts acts or words
however I order or translate the sound
spring is still coming, not even for me.

10.

a functional erection
blonde–imperial–
drunk
society!–a kill–half–
sunk
a fever starved–let die
                    –a section

no places trees or lies
no fir tree beech or
                         pine
the green grass and
                    the sea
the weather fine
two people–night–
time–   I slept
or I didn't

"our" intellect–earth
to the sky–
            the mineshaft
  the canary–the
nightingale–
                the shade
all night
complaining–tears

it's just that his heart
is fit to burst with
fizzy lemonade
    it's just as well to

fool around without a
life-raft
    you form us my
lord and then you
disappear

11.

It doesn't matter whether you stand in the sun or the shade
I can't see you, Donna, without conquering a touch of envy
                                        in myself
probably because you know how great my need is
every other desire has to cut me open to get in
while I bear the weight of my clear thoughts.
Another touch of envy or a hint of pity to ornament the vault
but since I trimmed you out of myself
my self became a bleached doily
and this is how I'm recycled.
A loving gaze collects three shadows on the lawn
the thing I wanted most of all was a mistake, a rude
                                        companion.
I declared the bicycle king and said yes to Saturday
                                        afternoon.
Thousands have a fever, let's build them palaces of ice
dripping with chandeliers of soft eye-light

12.

if this is my life – *la mia vita* – bitter torment under any tongue
if a man can squirm so much – I am too afraid to begin or end
the paralysis of these mornings will carry me into
my last years.
Whale, the light in your beautiful eyes is spent
and your personal blue arc of skin has turned silver
and Persephone has abandoned her droopy flower basket.
All the discoloured faces of artists stare at my daring,
they make me go scared and slow like a touched beetle.
Maybe the shapes of words can prop me up
that's why I'm searching amongst these gravestones.
There were the years, and the days, and the hours
but if time is relevant it's against all these beautiful desires.
I can make no oath that doesn't hold me to account
but perhaps I can make berries sprout in knots of wood,
slow late signs of life.

13.

From time to time as the geese fly north
you and the other whales slide between Rousay and Costa.
As much as each of them is less beautiful than you
so much the more does my tidal wave crest.

I bless the place, the time, and the hour. I am always doing that.
I am as innocent as a little boy kneading bread in
                                             golden slippers.
I bend my double-jointed arm wondering have I thanked
                                             God enough
for the tight back and busy head of the upright bird who can
                                             perch on a point.

From him, from the way he gets confused in tufts of grass
from his certain clicky feet and the triangles he knows in the
                                             sky
small flapping, tangerine beak

from him comes the smooth spirit
that scours you to the sky for every sexual feeling.
Yes, but I fly already, lifted by my hopes.

14.

Leaving my eyes behind
          I turn towards you all like in a horror movie
with the beautiful face of the one who is going to die.
I am so fucking free here, mine own John Poynz!
Only the ration betrays me. The garlic rule.
A sweet pickled beetroot can put an end to city thoughts.
The king today, see the loving way that he leads:
                    in the room / not in the room.
I step out to visit the portal of health, where the wind touches
                        the land. There's
an object less solid than whole: a spinal column under the bush
                    of sticks, some buds.
Women are made of small virtues
and little old pains, they come like crabs' pinches.
The hour of plants is at hand
take it. Don't refer to the things your mind knows but to what's
                        inside them.

Can you hear me?
Yes, I can really hear you.

15.

After I am caught doing cunnilingus
                    in the communal bed at law school
I am unapologetic with the professors
and I take comfort in your airy manner
which has them turning to one another and saying, "leave it".
Later in the imaginary greenhouse,
                    thinking again of the sweet good that I left
the long road ahead and the shortness of my life,
                         I am too horny for savasana
I stop the plants. I am unbigoted and clever.
There is a pair of weepy eyes in the soil down there.
A wagtail or a woodpecker assaults me in the foliage.
I develop a doubt: if I am a member of the spiritual sect
how come they allow me to live so far away?
A creepy baby texts me back: "have u forgotten
the privilege of lovers?
They don't need to be human."

16.

The old white cockerel moves himself
from the sweet place where he eggs his age
from the family that no longer uses plastic bags
from the dear father who will come to be missed
from indivisible labour and ancient fealty
from the extreme daylight of the backlit storm.
He would gladly help that old lady get the shopping in
broken by years and tired of walking
but instead he comes to Rome on a whim
kisses the curved spine of a young man
looks hopefully up at the sky
goes to the tailor for a blue silk suit.
Royal. He wonders how much more is possible
and then he sees you in your true form: green and shining,
        standing by

17.

Ram me on love – tears of the face
I must go to Flanders in a gale of sighs
io l'ho perduta! – I'm the tubular crescendo of a seal
wave rolls trifle with me – aqueous jelly and white curdled.
She's pregnant, and her sweet long-suffering smile
enlarges something in me – let's suffer together babe.
"Fuck my dad and everybody's dad.
I am the dad that nobody's had."
But my spirits unhouse me at the climax
when I come to the beginning of smooth action
pushing my fatal stars away from me
I stop before the finish line holding the key.
My soul rushes from my body to follow you
and my body, with many unique thoughts, wakes itself up.

18.

A huge snake chucked over the crescent moon
its forked slab of a tongue thudding into Sweden
its liver on fire with the light of an idea:
"there is a very hard struggle inside – between parts
when I die my heart will be divided ungratefully"
(don't squash the vegetables to give to the devil
she's already got plenty of teeth) out there in the dark
"I'm arriving and you have not noticed!
My legs are burning with the punches of death
I'm shitting out Shetland (this is a creation story)
come with me – don't come – come one by one –
come quietly, because you've killed the words
and their little bodies will make people cry
but I would like it if my tears sprouted alone."

19.

There are animals in the other world that will change
                              the way you see
if you will meet them instead of defending yourself.
Others whom this enlightenment offends
won't venture forth until evening approaches,
and others, crazed with hope,
will dance and joke in the fire. It is so splendid
to try another power. That of the arson?
The cowboy of my madness is in its final phase.
I am not strong enough to wait for the light
but how can I make myself stay
in dark places at late hours?
With shaky and dripping eyes,
this drives me to strike the match.
I know too well that what I want stands behind the fire.

20.

Growing a moustache and then feeling ashamed of it.
A beautiful incurious poet.
These things are lunar and recur so much so
it is what it is.
But I find I am weighed down. Not by my own arms,
or my big head on its stalk,
but by the cunning that it would take to ask
the deep questions of the moment.
Twenty times already my lips have opened
but my voice hovers, fluttering under my ribs.
I weep for Radvanovsky's Norma, her lips pulled sideways by
the force of score.

(This final verse is about how hard it is to write
but writing becomes, as it often will, wanking a dick.)
As for myself, *a foghorn in a man bun*, a creeping phlox, I'll go
big tonight.

21.

a thousand breaths	sweet warrior
peace	a woodlouse dropped on its back
I've offered	you don't want
your mind	is at the top of a hill
to hope	
	it's weak to hope
I disdain that	

it cannot be, ever again	such as it was
but now I flatten it	
in unhappy exile	any help is welcome
not knowing how to be alone	or how to make a phone-call
put a stop to	natural course
that heavy responsibility	let's use both our hands
too much the more of you	so much the more

22.

   for Dominic Sen

I'm not an animal but a guest of the earth
where I come from they hate the sun
time for work. how much is a day?
our sky blazes up your stars
we are desert empires. it's not good to hide in the wood
better to have a position in relation to the dawn

and aye, eye, I!   the beautiful dawn
she's gone and there's a shadow inside the earth
it's waking up the sleepy animals in the wood
it's now or never   lead with the sun
when I come telling tales about the stars
the dog is the guardian of the day

the evening scratches out the clear day
our darkness   others make the dawn
I look, thinking "these simple stars
that have made me aware of the sensual earth
soft on my skin I can feel the sun."
That puts me into the landscape: a man nourished by a wood.

I don't think she ever comes through the wood
but she does poison, whether by night or by day.
I like this one: the dog is the guardian of the sun.
I keep busy so I am not tired at the sounds of dawn
it would be so great to find her body on earth
oh my farm   I come from the stars

torn from you   my bright stars
down into the   cloying wood
leaving the body   a cover-up trite as earth
you'd see marks   up there one day
can recover   but here the dawn
can make me rich   as the rising sun

if only I was not alone at the sinking of the sun
and no one could see us but the stars, my bright stars!
I dream of one night for us all, and it would never be dawn,
and she wouldn't transform in the green wood
to escape me, like she did on the day
that what they call Apollo chased her into earth.

Even i will be buried in dry flakes of wood.
And the day will insult me with a. Rot of tiny stars
but. Trust me. Hurl the dawn into the sun.

23.

creation of parsley

    i.

In the sweetness of the first stage
he who hides, sees. It's all as green as grass
something grows in a type of time, the iron will, my bad.
Why sing the sickness that neutralises
I will sing as I see myself in freedom
while love disdains to stay in my hotel
then surely it is just like how he increases
too high   of that which predicts me
of those who are made the example of men.
Even if my hard scampi
was written off for a thousand penises
they're already tired of it, and in almost every valley
the sound of sighs is winding.
They seek to earn the trust of a virile life
and if memory won't help me here
sea urchins might   the torments
one thought remains but it is frivolous
everyone else is turning their back
it makes me sweet in my own strength.
I hold something inside me, I am the scourge.

ii.

I confess that from the very first sex
attack   many years have passed
so I have changed out of my youthfulness
and I am making ice creams in my heart:
mint, having almost adamantine qualities
distancing   left   hard
tears   not anymore   bathe my breast
nor break the sound. What I didn't possess
appeared to me to be a miracle in others
Alas, what the answer to who I am is not who I was
am I? What the end of life comes, loads up the evening
was I? sensing the crudeness of my reasoning
percussioning   strangulation
over the skirt   up-hitched

iii.

rudeness or a self-possessed woman
for whom little already never danced
cunning or strength or demanding an apology
I will transform into double that which I am
making myself a living man and a green laurel
in cold stations don't lose the layers
what makes me when   I first realize myself
in the metamorphosis of my person
a glimpse of my hat in some green fronds
they all hope to have for their crown
the feet are mossy and rooted
as every membrane responds to the spirit
daisies bloom over the woody earth
watered not by my inches but by a completely different river
my arms mutate woodily into two branches
nor does it distress me more
to find myself covered in white blossoms.
So this is how I protest and die
my hopes – as we know – mounted too high.

iv.

Because I didn't know where or when
anyone might find me alone and crying
by the well where a washed mistake might go
seeking inside the waters a sense of time
was already never then, my tongue not touched
I saw power and his malignant fall
from which I absorbed the colour of a swan.

Then I thundered along the lovely banks of drink
chattering and singing always
calling for mercy in a strange voice
lemonade sweet and wine-filled
this loving racket was designed
to humiliate my fierce-pipped heart
in the past that is, something recalled
but much more than that too, for, as they say,
from the sweetness comes the bitters.

v.

I have to say something
                         from the position that I'm in.
This evasiveness has infuriated all the animals
one of them lunges for my chest and grabs out my heart
saying understandably   "I can't make words out of this"
he divides it, dressing each part in its own outfit
so I don't recognise them. My sense of human!
The truth is an anorak's hood blown taut with wind
using TetraPak to body out my buzz in
a kaleidoscopic clutter-fuck of cowboy figurines
one of whom is secretly alive.   oh boy.

vi.

She spoke as her eyes misted up like car windows
and an earthquake ascended from tremors in the stone
I listened: "you don't have to read this but if you do"
she said: "please don't condemn me for my simplicity"

vii.

How I don't know, but you showed yourself independent
                    you are not as responsible as I am
I put everything there is between life and death
                        but because time is short
there's pressure, the lead breaks
        there are more things on my mind than are written
some trespass. I speak of it to someone
    they give out shiny medals to those who listen hardest.

viii.

Death becomes an urge to
pull up the potatoes with both of your hands
please give help to the afflicted virtues
the living voices that have been forbidden
to shout ink at this birthday card that will
                    anyway
                              get lost in the post
"I'm not even mine, I have no presents!"

ix.

I did believe her eyes
the indignity of doing that repaid my dignity.
this ball of dust was arduous to catch
it felt like tailor-made humiliation.
there's something about sepsis in your chart
were you ever bathed with a sponge?
who did you pray to when you wrote a poem?
looking for a reason roundabout the place
like someone who sleeps in back gardens
and wakes up one morning in grass shivering fragments.

x.

                                                    You
stand around accusing the evasive tabloid of your own
                                          thoughts
as some generic water swells the break between paving
                                          stones
that you always try to never step on
fall in and disappear under
                    I feel that with time I will come to be less
              bury me in a waterfall of pies while I smoke a pipe
clunky   make me humid and take me on a journey,
perhaps   do you dare to carry me to the baptismal font?
The manifestation of a speaking cunt
God will mix your spirits for you
you are already above all thanks
I want to haul you back into your maker
you wizened loaf of bread, you sage stuffing
you come blood yourself up in humble colours
and bow to me. To me?

xi.

Like a contrarian peacock / I sustain myself against your style
you then are eyeless, and I am a pack of sharpest needles
that had better not be repeated
one weird thing can give birth to so many others.

xii.

Porky Madonna is making a fuss
about miracles and the recognition of her life.
I think she is sick, inflating in the radius of pity.
It might be kind to let her go back home,
for nothing in the world could have prepared her for the faith of
                                                                    Men

which has more bone-breaking reprisals
more dryly turning away and scorning
and bottling up bits of you in ancient reliquaries
than the other option, which is to die without a name.

xiii.

A very painful and erroneous poltergeist wants me to remember
my pilgrimage of coins across the desert
but it was many years long and arduous
and it all came to a very bad end
and I returned to the damp earth
believing that that was the most pain I'd ever feel.

xiv.

I, Louise, followed my own desires
and through all the chatter
presented myself, beautiful and crude
naked in a fountain.
I was as strong as any rope.
I existed because I was incomplete.
I murdered shame, so they stopped to look.
in broad daylight
I sprayed cooling water on their faces
I said things that were true,
                        although they sounded like lies at the time
I drew myself in my own image
and though that was lonely as a marked deer
touch
me not   I translated myself from forest to forest
and felt even more myself as the siege on me intensified.

Song, you may be nothing more than a cloud of gold,
a fire suspended inside a book
                              a pube
but there turns out to have been an angel up in the air
wrapped in boiled cotton, lifted up
she knew a plague in 1564
I want to be her sweet little couverture
    and she knows it: *l'amour Lesbienne*

24.

take a branch and bend it round
put it on your head
now you are crowned. This crowning
unites us, even we who poetry

put it on your head
be a friend to your divas
nursing injuries from long ago
taking inventories of the bitter olive crop

now you are crowned. This crowning
you'll discover you're the foundling princess
loved and owned, exchanged for a pastoral amethyst

unite us, even we who in poetry
seek calmer springs of opiates
replenished: tale in mouth

25.

We are trekking on a purple sponge cake in an orange sky.
I point my feet east and west to make seedling prints
the quince rain is lavender, observes its own acidic effect
we collect golden butter oozing from its chosen nodes.
On the right-hand side, God walks in reverse
perverse heart tilted, hands upturned.
Adjourned my pretties, go home, say other prayers.
Layers spin out beneath us as the cake divides.
I fall into whipped cream, it's matte and black.
Crack shows me you, fallen through to piles of treasure.
Pleasure of blanched almonds pulverized along the way,
lazy toes flap in the wind. I am simply benevolent
event leading to event leading to event.
Spent countless hours of looking, no hell in sight.

26.

She struggles harder than me but does not see the land.
Battered and defeated she rides the waves, her hair grows.
The observant people dissolve their pity through telescopes
politely thanking the current that lands her floppy as fish.
She'll soon learn to fight more than to be captive
putting her mossy teeth to the cord around her neck
digging up vegetables with a burnt spatula
waging a very long war on the gentleman that stares.
Now all you people who praise her in triangular poems
addressed to the arbiters of amorous speech
                              do yourself the honour of stopping.
What greater glory is there than mercy, so spare us
and neither she nor I will mock you for changing.
One convert is worth 99 dyed in the wool problems.

27.

Charles V's successor and his bastard brother John

larping history under the banner of a burnt hot cross bun.

John sharpening the edge   Ali Pasha's head on a pike.
                                His sons, watching on.

Shamash-Shum-Ukin, Ashurbanipal, Taro, Jiro and Saburo,

Henry, Henry, Henry, G de A Munro (who shot his sons)

a gunshot snaps down the line to Alcazar.
                                A father is going in:

they are bloodstained; bloodstained with the blood

St Patrick sends hard words after Coroticus:

those people are alien to me and to Christ my God

all the highly-strung bookshelves breathe a sigh of relief:
                                alien to me, yes alien to me.

This and the uncontrollable anger of the talent pressed for time

all this has been put into fiery lumps in the bread

and as if I were the hole in Lindisfarne where stained glass
                                used to be

I'll devour it: *in nomine Patris et Filii*

28.

i.

this pie in the sky crusade is weather beaten it's true but we still scream for it in the name of the spirit of humanity and it dresses itself forth, not cramped and cowering but a hard and shiny Jeff Koons sex balloon of distorted vanity. Crusade, dilate for your God as obedient /slave-girls do, and if he is as bovine as your inferior brothers and if he turns his back on the chickpea world of your mothers

he does this to help you reach those far off better ports comforted by the premonition of a sugar wind from the west, sugar palaces nestled in some dark valley. We're obsessed with a valley so dark it will be lit only by our best thoughts, lashing us to an idea of chivalry that we must put to the test by the best and most direct route. Off to the true East we go! Heave ho and off, Argonauts!

But first the ritual: we must pray over ashes, drip sanctified
               tears
(beware that your eye beams don't get tied in a sideways love
               knot
it's the sort of Troilus that can happen in the ritual steam
but not in the Cruseyde where we can only count our
       merit points and prick ourselves hot)
this is outside of the normal run to eternal justice and we're
           switching gears
now let us turn our eyes to the ruler whose benevolence is so
             extreme
we are soft and damp and his hands stretch us up into a high
             scream.

Soon we'll hit the road, agile as deers. I turn my eyes in thanks
to where the breast of our new Charles is still leavening
the vengeance that delays the night delays the evening
and so for the dominion we dream of we stand deep breathing
           on the banks
clustering our minds as the panic of the crickets becomes
            deafening.
He stills them with the twitch of a word. In our daydream
         we are the blue shirts,
boding chem-death of the communists, the Babylonian rank,
and there'll be no blurred lines, to prevent a catholic own goal
           which hurts.

iii.

Every great house between Garona and the mountains
between Rodano and Reno and the salty waves
will swell the ranks of the Christian so-to-speak educator
bounding in truth and sweatily swinking to embalm the souls of
                                                    his /slaves
to exact his tribute from the Pyrenees to the last latifundium in
                                                    the mountains
to leave the shrines of Aragon in the spirit of their creators
to rekindle the ash of that phoenix on the new moors.

England, flush with island beauties bathing beside it,
                                    piqued by Scotland's mountains
will always support – in the sporting spirit – this horseplay of
                                                    mass graves
as long as it is far enough away that a butt joint can be called an
                                                    architrave
so to speak – of the Doric order that is – two-faced as any
                                    naughty old mountains.
Personally, I abide by the doctrine of the Helicon which says:
kick a rock and get a spring. Things get simple like that as we
                                    approach the equator
civilization reseeds. I did not say that this spring would be the
                                    source of drinking fountains
in act the print of my cruelty is reaching its height, I am
                                    Hercules, Ulysses, Homo Viator.

iv.

By what love are *you* licenced and dignified? My crusade is the very definition of love.

Which sons ever, which women, were made to a model as perfect as this?

One part of the world freezes under the suspension of snow,

there, in the brief snow driven days, some of our band gave in to the blue kiss

they became part of the stoical frieze, our temple historical, working hand in glove

to ensure that what we believe can be distinguished from the other things that we know

the adventurer and the pirate, the wholesale grocer and the ship owner, the gold digger and the merchant, appetite and force, and behind them, the baleful projected shadow of a form of civilization

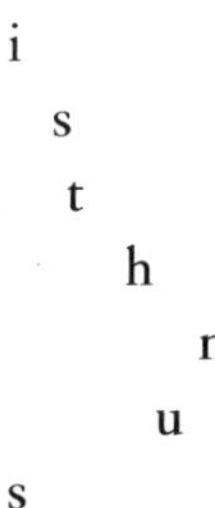

an arroba, bushel, pound, scruple, grain, manipulus, pugillus, pennyweight, groat, dram, spoon, cup, pint, quart, gallon, barrel, hogshead, puncheon, a butt, or a tun.

This is our scribblization writing its book. The noble paradox of Gawain to ponder: I have to but can't fuck you. Sche is schiny greene and schlinking over in a schatsuit, oof I'm schwellange! The order of the self-starter, a ballroom witticism, a series of mordant mysogestures, cloaks in puddles, the Carolingian knee bendeth to the noble rhythm of the centuries when Europe incubated Hitler and the Falange whilst decorating its dorm-room with shiniest 3D stickers of liberty encupidated in a honey boo boo recurrently haunted by this nightmare the liberalissimo has wetted the bed. Come, despite the muddles you can dip your wick into some leadership for no civilization, however ghost-ship, shall be rudderless.

The more faulty the logic the more it must be science-capsulated into a bone structure, a burning choo choo crossing the doodle of a partition, now that's what I call progress. Where the buck stops there's no telling. The knee cracketh, the knee inverteth, the humanist is a dingbell-chode: a disastrous clangy void indwelling but to his mind he is perfectly *imaginary executioners* and imaginary too are the /millions who – that's a cliché unworthy of those whose witness must be to understand the complexity of the thing – the /millions more who – paid their dues – whose resistant heat crisps the white man's burden to morality crumble – the /millions more who – it's the Platonic law that to be a man you must do the job that's already been done for you. Blackfriar, whitefriar, greyfriar, mendicant *encomenderos* in your counting house, do you dare to grumble?

about
belief
clever
because

about
constant
cleverness

about
blood
before
all

because
committed
and
clever

vii.

So now is the moment to wind your necks in
my gigolos and if you're angry, scream at the wind
it's your nostrils that keep you alive.
This is ok for the stomach-footed ones that have slimed
their way to the top and sealed themselves in for dinner.
Holding hostage is the available job from 9 to 5
but that is the question, to survive or not to survive.

You could also try some language, some inky praise
to get a patron, but unless you are Orpheus or Amphion
you may as well throw Jesus by the pigtails it's so wrong
so stick to your guns son, maybe ask for a raise.
I know you're nostalgic for the sound of a clear sermon
there never were occasions so beautiful or smooth to run
maybe save up for a good thesaurus and see what it says.
It says our crusading days are done.

you see the death of husbands and the lost women all clothed in
                                                    brown
not for this miserable ruin of the people of the east did we raise
                                                    the dead
but for the mortal narrowness that defends itself in a copse of
                                                    trees
and sticks it to thousands of others unseen, although herd and
                                                    read.
Why inch toward
                      why convene there in the circuit of the crown
you can take the knees out of the mind but you can't take the
                                                    mind out of the knees.
Your years preserved you for so much good. Go in piece old man
                                                    and keep your bees.

You will see Italy and the honoured shore
once more, that was concealed to me as I fought
no sea   no mud   no smoke I sought
only love that with his searchlight on the moor

now vaporizes me where most he lights me up. I thought
that in nature you can be not what you've dressed up as.
That's why, as a fugitive, I am naked and I go on all fours.
But the roots of the things I have killed stare at me from under
                                                    the grass.

29.

Green bloody clothes, dark or lost,
    Don't you dare dress this unique lady
    Not in your golden hair or blonde tresses tied
  So beautiful like the ones that tell me
To arbitrate in the freedom streets.
    Dryly she pulls me such that I cannot support
    Any yoke that's less heavy
  And even if she arms herself to hurt herself
The spirit from which comes the lack
    Consigns me to where the suffering gathers force.
    Call her: "she of the unbridled desire
  Suddenly perceived" that ravishes me from the heart
Every delirium print and every indignity
    She sees herself reflected in a glass of wine.
    However much she already suffers for love
  She's ready to suffer more
Until her heart is confined to the same sanitorium as her killer.
    Damn rust of mercy that envelops me
    Vengeance will come, if only as protection from
                            humiliation
  Pride and anger are the steps I take to move
Don't close the door and don't lock it.
    The hour and the day that I lost the light
    In the beautiful black and the beautiful white
  That fattens me up for where love runs
Clear from this pink life that coddles me.
    There were roots in those whom age
    Looked to cut, they were rotund and long.
  Seeing who doesn't pave the way in lead or wood
Tears then from the well-read eyes
    By them that in the back of the lack

By the side of my bath, first pulled themselves tight.
Little painting. I can't rouse myself from the want
That faces me in a just part of the sentence
For her breath, her spirit and her dignity
It washes her pages.
My thoughts don't make themselves different from me
(so much already that) I tire myself out
The beloved flat thing in her own contortions
In that I pray that however they collect me up
They are at least directed to the sky by every way
And doesn't have aspirations to travel
Arbitrarily in a more salted boat.
Kind stars who make answers of themselves
To the fortunate faithful ones
When the beaten hill sinks down there into the undergrowth.
What is star on earth?   And how in laurel sheathed?
Protect little green, the prayer of honesty
Where it doesn't expand no fog in the din
And never an aggravating wind.

my thoughts have become alien to me

I know well that a want enclosed in verses
Will be praised until it is tired of itself.
Who graces the hand to write such things?
A scattered cellist, her spine, the memory which recollects her?
How much power it scans?   How much beauty?
Which eyes reflect sign of all bravery?
What is sweeter than my key-locked heart?
How much the sun turns over to cost me more dearly?
Still no greeting from you, woman.

30.

31.

This gentle animal, I want for it to be a horse.
It's called to another life by its own mechanism (that's
sickness, it's just a question of gradations from the most
blessed part). If captured there's no reason it couldn't be
a horse
even if that would distort sumnthing
because to look at her infinitely you'd think she could be
anything. The souls around her are scattered and that
that movement of hers like a ripple through nothing
that shimmy of time, a syncopated ticking under the fourth
beat
that tenebrosity boxed into a mirror and melted in a green flash
is the utmost of things. And that only should have the fame and
the shout.
But it will be nothing (in that it could be all). She won't inhabit
herself
she never did. She died of headaches. If she flies any higher
than this I swear
I'll be so grapefruit I'll dye myself.

32.

what sort of an extremist (*people also search for: Immigration*)

looking at a rainbow dancing through a droplet on a white cloth
regrets sewers?

Not Peter Kemp, *distinguished irregular soldier* (21 minutes
of oral history on the

Imperial War Museum website *thereafter*) *retained his nose*
for and against fascism

but his *loyal friend* Captain Gonzalo de Aguilera

his English education, a white face made bulbous in the
cave of a silver spoon.

It's something like hard imprisonment under a heavy layer of
fish.

*had we no sewers in Madrid, Barcelona and Bilbao, all these
Red leaders*

would have died in their infancy instead of exciting the rabble

Is it the extent or the logic of the human that's the problem?

Can it be fixed if the wheels on the dubious   go round

It all comes clear like sticky glue, softly washing the limbs of
the dead

but if they are still living, do something

33.

The stars were still on fire, but I would not say "amorously".
In the west the propitious one who makes Juno jealous
was hovering over Costa Head and brighter than all the others
she twisted and turned and sparkled her light.
She was up-hoisted, little old thing, on *the noose of your curl*
a gem disintegrating and unshod in relation to carbon
(the pungent lovers, at this stage covered in blood,
still called to each other out of habit in teary voices).
When I brought my spray of green grasses to the graveyard
to be added into the heart's decision, used and passed by
I was dosed with dreamgrams until the pain softened.
Now I am much changed, quite different from before.
Some would say I've lost my grip, but not on
Venus. I won't be torn from you.

34.

for Cecilia Giménez

                              If Apollo still lives

he's some warmth in the tessellating waves.
I have loved hairy girls who are
still trapped in altarpieces – raised in oblivion
from laziness of fresco and bitter laughable time
that lasts however much the face absconds itself
defended and dishonoured by the busy paintbrush.

restoration   restoration   restoration

by the power of the loving hope that spoils things

that sustains you in bitter life

this print in the unerasable air   funny,

by some marble we see each other again and again.

Remember when you used to lie down on the grass

and I would stretch my arms out over you, making shade?

35.

I pace more and more thoughtfully on the blank wall

measuring the slow steps of each of my legs

like oars of a galleon on a vertical sea to carry the spices,

except that I've escaped the piratical intention.

I find no other scheme that tickles me half as much

as to tread in fourteeners on the bourgeois manifest(o of these people)

their acts of happiness exhausted in another custard cream.

From outside it reads as if I am a vampire inside

from inside I believe myself at home. So be my guests.

The mountains and the shores, the rivers and the forests of the house.

Damp is the temper of my life: slow, unless accelerated by a flick.

Thoughtful antennae spread-eagled, little dancing in a selvedge

of their woven stuff, looking. I don't know that kind of love,

but I know myself.

36.

Phil
if death would acquit us
of the crime by which we're floored
we'd already be red-handed, digging down
to bury these tedious members in the ground flesh.
But it would be like throwing the frying pan into the fire
we'd still be cooking meat sauce! Anyway, we're singing this
for you, *a man that walks painfully, hard put to it to move.*
If it's revenge you want, now's the time to launch
the final arrow from your borrowed bow.
Ignore Zeno, this one'll hit the mark.
Oh and Neoptolemus
You cannot just
opt out

Skin 1

Yes, the thread is weak and she hangs on it, the whole weight of my life. Somebody help my once and future wife. My dunce and stupid wife is dancing on the line. The executive empire leaves a knife cutting holes in our sweet will. Still, she hangs, my one true lantern. "Ding dong the witch" they sang. She was alight on that occasion and I went blind, skewered on the straightness in her spine. Truly it was a sorry sight but support yourself, sad soul. A cut kite can, in tighter times, return.

A piece of time hardens in me. I burn and leave an amber rock of ashes that contains my lives. This is by design. What century am I in? Look.

Skin 2

Time passes and the hours are so prompt and ready to supply the journey that I don't spend enough time with my attorney even to count how much I'm running to death days. Only just puncturing the east, the sun on a gurney without our help won't make it across the swamp to the competing horizon, where its mouth is stopped. Although they take the long way our lives are just as short. Fingers so spindly they slip the net, a body so heavy and frail. Yes, we know, we know now. A face so pale I can't discover how it's related as blood and skin separate finger peels itself from nail and eggshell eyelids crack to blue it comes unstuck because it wasn't true.

Skin 3

Thanks a bunch for your fugal wisdom mortality visions. I was looking for a syncopation to dance me out of these flares. Hey there lover [the short sharp whistles type, dexterous with breasts and between thighs, the sweet puddings type, a folding over, a hard man self-exiled by yelps and strummed elisions to the rough end of his fingertips] my crinoline, my pin cushions kicked to the curb. A river flowing with no rests in water I play to my own lights and all my darknesses I gather my breath to petticoat the bathers for the ball where by glow of firefly they are bolting in the coracles. After all there's a reel calm in the halfway of the gods. Consulting oracles a penny drops in the control rods and something bites me in the great hall; I don't react at all. It's a joyful life but it only takes one fool to find something bad suspended in the swimming pool.

Skin 4

I am relieved. A slapping beat refreshes me. I was born on the same day that they saw Venus bring her fish to fry. A new breath on the mini mouth organ and no containment for my mind. Mother river runs me to the sea to nets of olives getting sweet. I bang dextrose to the drum and squiggles of sun on my bare bum. My fat baby mer-personality is totally disburdened of reality. Unmoored. Want it to last but had one too many ice creams too fast. Nurse! Bounce me back to hilarity and put on my silky socks. Tomorrow I shit bomb the alarm clock.

new pleasure of the cunning human in herself that something
she has found to do is to love a thing new: some soft colt ham
of collected sighs. I am one of those whom weeping afflicts
it's true, and never half as good as when I outwit myself with
tears – when impregnated – the doctor of health does a tour
de forceps in the heart of the labour a little head that tempts
him in to bad behaviour reasoning from the known to the
unknown but that's not what it is that touches me to groan.
To feel if she does something inside I run back and re-enter by
the wide trapdoor in the jaw of my mind and the unmanned
heart is punished delicately by the head

that through the streets of my love they would me lead

Skin 6

The pigtails of gold bunched on the sun, the curling tongue, the warming iron, what's done is done. In short be bold, be rooted in the world, be not too bold. I have already been, by a courteous lion, mistaken for a counterfeit pea coat to try on any more epaulettes could lead to capital armaments side parting the kind of angelic greeting that would unseat him. Lovely to have a reachable want of sense, one that I don't dare to think till the high blood drags me into it and by crying more with more dilation of the gossamer gloved waving hands and the canting arms, the different clans and their smoothly different actions put into effect their sweet disdainful (otherwise humble) plans and the beautiful young breasts go heaving in the station where towering intellect meets plain old frustration and quickens them off to these places of alps and iron. I don't know if I will go or wait. The scion of a noble house has shown an interest in getting me undressed. Something is edging open that I don't know how to shut; the empty house resounds flatly in the hollow gut. I've gone my way. I think it best. Courtesy rents a cottage with a view. I think that I should rent one too.

Skin 8

Song, always the last one singing

"O naked spirit of the man of flesh and bone!"

I mistranslated Petrarch's lyric poems from Italian into English every day from March to May 2020, until I got to number 37. The edition I used was *Petrarch's Lyric Poems*, translated by Robert M. Durling, Harvard University Press, 1976.

Later, I rewrote the mistranslations until they became poems in a struggle with their genealogy, trying not to know that there was ever anyone else behind them. They seek themselves in the definition of Petrarch's poems but because they are constitutionally unfaithful and solipsistic, they only lose Petrarch's poems in themselves.

If this is a process that deserves its own name, I want to call it erotic translation. Within the object of my knowledge there is always the object of my desire. This is neither innocent nor pure. Within what I knew of Italian there was always what I wanted to be knowing, what I was already missing. This wanting (of which I am, of course, ashamed) created poems as edges holding space for other poems. But no poem ever concedes its space entirely. I mean that my own desire formed the edges of the poems in this book, but it does not finally clarify for me who wrote them or to whom they were written.

Petrarch's book was originally titled in Latin: *Rerum Vulgarium Fragmenta,* or fragments of common things. Many fragments have been drawn into this book too and I've collected some of them here in the tradition of a commonplace book (I gather Petrarch may have called this a *zibaldone*). Think of it as a garnish that justifies the parsley, if not the space. Quotations that appear within the poems themselves are in italics. Uncredited text comes from the margins of my green translation notebook. A few of the poems have become spaces for further creations and this is noted. Many voices do not explicitly appear although they have been incredibly important to this book. Two are: Verity Spott's *Poems of Sappho* and Sophie Seita's *Lessons of Decal*.

Thank you to everyone who has been with *Space Parsley* already and with me as I wrote it, to Ella Mahony for its cover, and to the87press – Azad, Kashif, Sopo, Aisheshek and Stani – for making it into a book. I am also grateful to the editors of *Blackbox Manifold* for publishing poem "23" in Issue 24. And so, let's scatter:

"garnish, v. *transitive*. To furnish (a place) with means of defence; to garrison; to supply with men, arms, and provisions. *Obsolete*."
    – Oxford English Dictionary

"She has managed to design a new order (or disorder) for the premises of the brain's center for speech. She is an excellent interior designer"
    – Yoko Tawada, in Sophie Seita and Uljana Wolf, *Subsisters*

"Desire makes its entry with the general collapse of the question, what does it mean?"
    – Deleuze and Guattari, *Anti-Oedipus*

"Beyond the superficial, the considered phrase, "It feels right to me," acknowledges the strength of the erotic into a true knowledge, for what that means is the first and most powerful guiding light toward any understanding."
    – Audre Lorde, *Uses of the Erotic: The Erotic as Power*

"From the flesh out, it seems, Archilochus understands the

law differentiating self from not-self, for Eros cuts into him just at the point where that difference lies. To know desire, to know words, is for Archilochus a matter of perceiving the edge between one entity and another."

    — Anne Carson, *Eros: The Bittersweet*

"I think she has a certain masochistic-sadistic erotic engagement with the philosophers. [...] But I do worry that her aggressive engagement was in some sense a function of her attachment to these texts."

    — Judith Butler, "The Future of Sexual Difference"

"Shame, it might finally be said, transformational shame, *is performance*."

    — Eve Kosofsky Sedgwick, *Touching Feeling*

"Bill laughed, 'Well, do you feel that your work accomplishes what ... ever you set out to do?'
'How am I supposed to decide that? [...] Maybe, just, I did it.' Kid sat back. 'And maybe, you know, other people can think of reasons not to even insist on that too much.'"

    — Samuel R. Delany, *Dhalgren*

"I cannot but think (if what I have writ answers the Intention it was writ with) the Subject of the following Papers very well merited those few Houres that were bestow'd upon 'em."

    — Damaris Cudworth Masham, *Discourse Concerning the Love of God*

"Like his favorite book, the Confessions, Petrarch's love poetry examines the experience of not being able to want what one wants to want, to know what one really wants, or to stop wanting what one does not want to want."

    — Melissa Sanchez, *Queer Faith*

"In other words parsley gets things going, it breaks up
congestion and keeps things moving along."
   – Maud Grieve, *A Modern Herbal*

1.

"Quand vous lirez, ô Dames Lionnoises,
Ces miens escrits pleins d'amoreuses noises,
Quand mes regrets, ennuis, despits et larmes
M'orrez chanter en pitoyables carmes,
Ne veuillez pas condemner ma *simplesse*,
Et jeune erreur de ma fole jeunesse"

["Oh, women of Lyon, whenever you read
these writings of mine, so full of love and need –
all the worries, grudges, tears, sobs, and regret
that the piteous music of these songs has set –
please don't condemn me for simplicity
because of my youthful weakness."]

   – Louise Labé (1522-1566), "Elégie 3", translated by
     Annie Finch (2006)

4.

"Has Blue Whale ever been recorded in Orkney?"

"I have a couple and two vertebrae that I found on the
shore near the Martello tower on Hoy, 20 odd years ago –
the largest disc is 31cm across. – who lived near there and
worked on the Otter Bank, the bank boat, said he could
remember it coming ashore in the 1920's when he was a

wee boy and how his dad had helped butcher it and brought whale meat home for dinner!"

"A possible Blue Whale was stranded at Longhope in either 1883 or 1884 – Buckley and Harvie-Brown (in Sillocks, Skarfies and Selkies, 2005)"

— "Orkney Cetacean Group", Facebook.

5.

"uncover your curls of ambergris, so the entire world
may be perfumed"

— Zeyneb Hatun (early 15th century), "Remove Your Veil", translated by Najaat Black in *Ottoman Lyric Poetry* (1997)

7.

I've been getting the date wrong.

8.

"Leeve mooder, leet me in!
Lo, how I vanysshe, flessh and blood and skyn!"

— Chaucer, *The Pardoner's Tale*

9.

March 26th 2020 – today 8pm, clapping for the NHS – I
was born 420 years and 1 day after the Battle of Lepanto.

Altrui: of another, indefinite pronoun

10.

Mary's birthday – beautiful sun – breakfast outside –
couldn't wake up – dreams – angry.

Costei: Tuscan pronoun, this one or that one or she, or this
thing that is yours

"Dr Larry Brilliant, an epidemiologist who is a veteran
of the eradication of smallpox, and is now the chairman
of an organization called Ending Pandemics, warned that
if Trump sends everyone back to work by Easter "I think
history would judge it an error of epic proportions",
        –   New York Times, March 26 2020.

12.

reading Virginia Woolf – afraid I'll not make the things I
want to make – afraid of other people's seriosity and mine –
last night – full of love – felt like nobody

"Later [parsley] became associated with Persephone who
guided the souls of the dead to the underworld and was
used to decorate the tombs and graves of the dead, in hopes
of pleasing her. Later, Christians replaced Persephone with

St Peter, but maintained the connection between parsley and
guidance of the soul. Parsley can take 2-4 weeks to start
from seed. An old folk legend explains that parsley has to
go to Hades and back 9 times before it will germinate."
 – Maud Grieve, *A Modern Herbal*

13.

Bea Addis, Joseph Minden and I devised and recorded a
'madrigal' of this poem, which we called "Him".

At a particularly magic iteration of Horseplay, the monthly
poetry night run by Ben Graham and Verity Spott in
Brighton, a group of us sang "Him" as a round.

You can listen to both versions at kataddis.com/space-parsley

15.

the dream of cunnilingus in the communal bed – the law
professor – too horny – cat and mouse – pied wagtail or
white wagtail or hummingbird

"Yoga has been put in an ironic position: Colonized
and commodified, a tradition rooted in detachment and
equanimity has been hijacked by a grasping possessiveness. I
titled my work #*WhitePeopleDoingYoga*."
 – Chiraag Bhakta, *Mother Jones*, October 17th 2019

16.

incredible storm – light sun waves crashing back into
themselves – whether to vote – Edinburgh festival cancelled
– need to call some of my friends!

17.

Don Carlo – Verdi – who says <u>bravo?</u>

"io l'ho perduta"
>   –   Don Carlo, dir. Nicholas Hytner at the Met, Dec
>   11th, 2010

18.

making slate raised beds – happiest day – eating tons of eggs
– body so tired – desperate for J to love my poems

"In its dying agony the Stoor Worm shot out its huge forked
tongue so high that it caught hold of the moon. It would
have pulled it from the sky but the fork of its tongue slipped
over the horn of the moon and it came back down to earth
with a thundering crash, leaving a huge hole in the surface of
the world. Water poured into the hole and it cut off the land
of the Danes from Norway and Sweden. There it remains to
this day as the Baltic Sea, and if you look at a map you can
still see the great forks of the Stoor Worm's tongue.

[...]

A giant went to Norway to cut peats and he filled his

basket and set off for home. As he waded through the sea
he needed to answer the call of nature, so he dropped his
trousers and in her words, he "shet land", and that was
how Shetland was made. He carried on, but the strap of his
basket broke and all his peats landed in the sea, and that's
how Orkney was made."

  –   *Orkney Folk Tales*, by Tom Muir (2014)

19.

BEL CANTO – Norma by Bellini

20.

"a foghorn in a man bun"
  –   review of Norma at the Met, by James Jordan,
       The Observer, 26th September 2017.

21.

<u>yes</u> today – yesterday

       Collective Poem 21

My fiat, so sweet takes me everywhere
glitter stains, for you! I forever go at your pace
to the heart, send it back, as you don't care for me any longer
to watch as we fish, we drink Superior
And then I told you about the beautiful sphere

Live in hope, they say, as if it is weakness to do anything less.
As if hope right now isn't, in some part a lie.
Sitting between spaces, find something of indignation
Or so the scabs in the heart not found in the voice are led to
make you

believe in the easy fidelity of other lovers' sorceries
poor man led by surface only
I hate to think what you're missing
this heavy fault seems ambiguous to all of us:
it's wanting more than there is to want

—   This is a collective erotic translation of Petrarch's poem 21, written by Christen Douressaeu, Avani Jurakhan, Viktoria Lien, Ariana Nazario, Kiara Royce, Morgan Smith, Ellie Stimpson, Jennifer Wei, Anna Moser, and me, during Anna Moser's class at New York University, *The Lyric Condition*, on Friday September 18th 2020

22.

This poem has become "My Stars", a song written and recorded by Alex Cohen (aka Dominic Sen) and Edward Lyle Barton (kataddis.com/space-parsley)

"the dog is the guardian of the tree: canis arboris custos est"
   —   Latin exercise

"And Daphne, the goddess translated,
In all her sense grown laurel, wants you transformed to a wind"
   —   Rilke, Sonnets Part Two, XII, translated by
       Stephen Cohn, (2000).

Aneurin Bevan and Clement Attlee – the "royal fifth" –
huge savannah empires + small forest communities

"others were moaning most bitterly, gazing towards heaven,
fixing their eyes upon it, as if they were asking for help
from the father of nature – others struck their faces with the
palms of their hands"
> – G.E. Zurara (1453-54) in Robin Blackburn, *The
> Making of New World Slavery*

23.

"*creation of parsley*"
> – Diane Di Prima, "Babylonia"

"*Alas, what am I? What was I?*"
> – Petrarch, Poem 29, translated by Robert M.
> Durling

"*touch me not*"
> – From the Latin *noli me tangere*, John 20:17.
> Caesar apparently inscribed this phrase on the
> collar of his deer, Thomas Wyatt refers to it in
> "Whoso List To Hunt", and it haunts Spenser's
> *Amoretti*, 67.

"*l'amour Lesbienne*"
> – Louise Labé, "Elégie 1", translated by Annie Finch

24.

He was standing on a slightly raised rock to survey his flock

survey his flock and was directing them to their
pasturages by the notes of his transverse flute.
The sheep seemed to hearken and to regulate
their pace by the pasturing signals of the pipes.
One would imagine that their heavy fleeces were
of gold; this effect was not produced artificially,
but the native ruddiness of the amethyst tinted
the backs of the sheep. The light frolicking of
lambs was also represented. Some scampered
up the rock in a troop, others gamboling friskily
about the shepherd gave the rock the appearance
of a rustic theater. Some wantoning in the flame
of the amethyst as in the sun bounded over the
rocks on the tips of their hooves. The rock was
not counterfeit but real; at the edges of the stone
the artist had marked off the space he desired,
thinking it otiose to feign stone in stone. Such was
that ring.

  — from Heliodorus, *An Ethiopian Romance*,
translated by Moses Hadas

25.

"stand at the touch hole of the bombard with lighted match
in one hand" João de Barros, quoted by Robin Blackburn in
The Making of New World Slavery.

27.

"anyone who does not gather with me, scatters"
Matthew 12:30

crusade declared by Philip VI in 1334

*"they are bloodstained: bloodstained with the blood [...]
those people are alien to me and to Christ my God"*
     –   St Patrick's letter to Coroticus.

28.

Jonathan Riley-Smith, "Crusading as an Act of Love",
History, 65 (1980).

"However, the most well-known foreign volunteers to fight
for Franco were the seven hundred Blue Shirts of the Irish
battalion under General Eoin O'Duffy. [...] For most of
them this was no more or less than a religious crusade [...]
the battle of Christianity against Communism [...] disaster
followed and their first casualties were inadvertently at
the hands of the Francoists. At the battle of the Jarama
in February 1937, one of their companies was fired on
by a Falangist unit which mistook them for International
Brigaders"
     –   Paul Preston, *The Spanish Civil War* (2006).

*"the adventurer and the pirate, the wholesale grocer and the
ship owner, the gold digger and the merchant, appetite and
force, and behind them, the baleful projected shadow of a
form of civilization"*
     –   Aimé Césaire, Discourse on Colonialism (1950)
            translated by Joan Pinkham (2000)

Edward III – order of garter 1348 – "on y soit qui mal au
pense" [shame on him who thinks ill of it]

"[t]hey would now not only come to overrepresent
their conception of the human (by means of a sustained
rhetorical strategy based on the topos of iconicity [Valesio
1980]) as the human, thereby coming to invent, label, and
institutionalize the indigenous peoples of the Americas
as well as the transported enslaved Black Africans as the
physical referent of the projected irrational/subrational
Human Other to its civic-humanist, rational self-
conception."
    – Sylvia Wynter, "Unsettling the Coloniality of
      Being/Power/Truth/Freedom" (2003)

Etymology of Orpheus: servant/slave/orphan or, to change
allegiance, or best voice.

29.

"my thoughts have become alien to me"
    – Petrarch, Poem 29, translated by Robert M.
      Durling.

30.

This is a call for submissions! Write poem 30 – it could be
anything in any form that you feel fills the space in the book,
or it could be a response to Petrarch's original poem 30 in
Rime Sparse – and submit it to poemthirty@gmail.com

At some point, this could become its own book.

31.

"I grant that all creatures are originally one Substance, from the lowest to the highest, and consequently convertible or changeable, from one of their Natures into another" – "every Creature is Material and Corporeal; yea, Matter and Body itself; and by consequence the most Noble Actions thereof, are either Material and Corporeal, or after a certain Corporeal manner." – "Earth thou art, and unto Earth thou shalt return [...] hath no less a Spiritual than a Literal Signification" – "But now the Foundation of all Love or Desire, whereby one Thing is carried unto another, stands in this, That either they are of the same Nature and substance with them, or like unto them, or both" – "there remains yet something of Universal Love in all Creatures, one towards another [...] which certainly must proceed from the same Foundation, viz. in regard of their First Substance and Essence, they were all one and the same Thing"

> – quotations from Anne Conway, *The Principles of the Most Ancient and Modern Philosophy* (first published anonymously, 1690)

"one first matter all,
Indu'd with various forms, various degrees
Of substance, and in things that live, of life:
But more refin'd more spirituous, and pure,
As nearer to him plac'd or nearer tending"
> – Milton, *Paradise Lost*, 5.472-6

"My brain I'll prove the female to my soul,
My soul the father, and these two beget
A generation of still-breeding thoughts;
And these same thoughts people this little world
In humours like the people of this world."
> – Shakespeare, *Richard II*, 5.5.6-10

32.

"people also search for: Immigration"
  –   Google

"Loyal friend, fearless critic and stimulating companion that
he was, I sometimes wonder if his qualities really fitted him
for the job he was given of interpreting the nationalist cause
to important strangers. For example, he told a distinguished
English visitor that on the day the Civil War broke out he
lined up the labourers on his estate, selected six of them
and shot them in front of the others – '*Pour encourager les
autres*, you understand.'
　　　　He had some original ideas on the fundamental
causes of the Civil War. The principal cause, if I remember
rightly, was the introduction of modern drainage."
  –   Peter Kemp, quoted in Paul Preston, *The Spanish
      Civil War.*

"Peter Kemp was *a distinguished irregular soldier* during
the Second World War, and long retained his nose for
trouble spots thereafter."
  –   Obituary in *The Independent*, 4th November 1993

"Sewers caused all our troubles. [...] Had we no sewers in
Madrid, Barcelona, and Bilbao, all these Red leaders would
have died in their infancy instead of exciting the rabble and
causing good Spanish blood to flow."
  –   Captain Gonzalo de Aguilera's theory of the
      Spanish Civil War, quoted in Paul Preston, *The
      Spanish Civil War.*

33.

"Does the one hanging
        by *the noose of your curl*
        touch his feet to the ground?
With delight
        he surrenders his life
        twisting,
        twirling."

        –   from an untitled poem by Nejâtî (d.1509),
             translated by Najaat Black in *Ottoman Lyric Poetry.*

almus-a-um (Latin) – nourishing, cherishing, bountiful,
propitious.

34.

I am maniacally driven to only communicate in herb-jokes
to my oldest friends & infuriated and cut to the quick when
they don't respond in kind – but what am I looking for? A
meeting of minds?

35.

She returns to the disdainful rind – woodlouse sonata.

36.

un varco (italian) – passage – spinto – shot

Hush! I hear a footfall,
footfall of *a man that walks painfully.*
Is it here? Is it here?
I hear a voice, now I can hear it clearly,
voice of a man, crawling along the path,
hard put to it to move. It's far away,
but I can hear it; I can hear the sound well
the voice of a man wounded; it is quite clear now.

    – Sophocles, *Philoctetes*, translated by David Grene

37.

NAKED FLESHY BODY POEM – to have the courage to
be corrected, or to change – I'm looking for the edge, I said.
I'm looking for the edge.